PIANO • VOCAL • GUITAR

THE BIRTH OF ROCK & ROLL

FROM RHYTHM AND BLUES TO ROCKABILLY...
FROM THE ROOTS OF ROCK TO ELVIS

COVER BACKGROUND: WESTLIGHT

ISBN #0-88188-995-4

7777 West Bluemound Road P.O. Box 13819 Milwaukee, WI 53213

Copyright © 1991 Hal Leonard Publishing Corporation.
International Copyright Secured All Rights Reserved

For all works contained herein:
Unauthorized copying, arranging, adapting, recording or public performance for profit is an infringement of copyright.
Infringers are liable under the law.

CHRONOLOGICAL CONTENTS

*Indicates Rhythm & Blues Chart

ALPHABETICAL CONTENTS

781.66
H629
c 1

THE BIRTH O ROCK & ROL

ROCK... IT WAS BORN IN THE U.S.A., AN OUTGROWTH OF RHYTHM AND BLUES, A PURELY AMERICAN SOUND THAT'S NOW GLOBAL. (IN FACT, IT'S GALACTIC AS VOYAGER I AND II LEAVE THE SOLAR SYSTEM PLAYING STRAINS OF CHUCK BERRY FOR ANY ALIEN LIFE FORM WITHIN EARSHOT OR SENSORY PERCEPTION.)

Many credit a 1951 rhythm and blues (R&B) recording, "Rocket '88," by Ike Turner as the first rock recording. Pianist/guitarist Turner and his group, the Delta Rhythm Kings, recorded this tune in Memphis on the Chess label with the wild and rough sound of saxophonist Jackie Brenston and an overamplified, fuzzed, electric guitar of Link Wray. The guitar sound is said to be the result of an amp speaker cone being stuffed with paper by Sam Philips (see "The King") after it was damaged falling off Turner's car on the way to the session.

"Rocket 88" was subsequently covered (cover — a new recording of an original recording) by a western swing band, Bill Haley and the Saddlemen. Haley and his band were beginning to cross their western swing style with R&B, and in 1952 with his rename band, the Comets, they released "Rock The Joint." This was followed by "Rock A-Beatin' Boogie" which had the lines "Rock, rock, rock everybody; roll, roll, roll everybody."

Haley had been playing midwestern high school dances for years. He had seen how the big band beat was no longer cutting it for the teens. Instead the teens were sneaking off to the black clubs, listening to black radio stations and picking up the wilder dances well as black expressions, such as "go, man, go" or "crazy, man, crazy." In 1953, "Crazy, Man, Crazy" was the first rock song to enter the national charts; then Haley's cover of Joe Turner's "Shake, Rattle And Roll" went top ten in 1954. In 1955, they released "Rock Around The Clock" – a combination R&B and Southern-influenced rock sound that became known nationwide via the film *Blackboard Jungle*. Its success was wi and it is touted in rock annals as the first "white" rock 'n' roll hit.

It was Cleveland D.J. Alan Freed who named rock and roll. Freed was heavily educat in music and a trained radio engineer; it's said that he "lived every beat of every note of the music he played." He saw the trend white teens buying R&B records at a local record store, and as early as 1951, he'd begun programming R&B tunes to his main white teenaged audience. In '52, he stage an all-Black R&B concert in Cleveland to a sold-out, racially mixed audience.

LITTLE RICHARD AND BILL HALEY

"Rock and roll" was an old sexual blues term that popped up in many R&B tunes. O story goes that when Freed picked up Bill Haley's "Rock A-Beatin' Boogie," he went crazy over the first line. However even earli "rock and roll" did occur in the lyric of the Dominoes' "Sixty Minute Man" and the Clovers' "Ting-A-Ling." It was Freed's radio program, *The Moon Dog Rock 'n' Roll Hou Party,* that finally kicked open the doors to rock and roll by bringing rhythm and blues to a broad young audience and talking directly to them. In addition, Freed's move to radio stati WINS in New York, and the rock concerts he produced throughout the country (plus sever rock and roll-based movies) brought rock and roll to the attention of the entire country.

Another camp feels that the Crew-Cuts' 1954-cover of the Chords' R&B hit, "Sh-Boom signaled in the rock era because of its enormous success. It certainly opened the charts ıany groups whose distinctive group harmonies and use of nonsense syllables later became ıown as *doo wop*. (See the section on "Doo Wop" in *History of Rock – The Early 60s*.)

1956 was an incredible year for rock. Elvis Presley crossed over to the pop charts from ıe country and western (C&W) charts, and Chuck Berry, Little Richard and Fats Domino ·ossed over from the R&B charts. All of these rock forerunners took their cue from black ues and various forms of country music; especially true to these roots were Sam Phillips' :rew" of artists which included Elvis Presley.

'HE SUN ALSO RISES

Sam Philips was an amazing man. A former radio engineer and announcer, ꜱ started his Memphis Recording Service for black artists who wanted to ·cord and "just had nowhere to go." Initially, he recorded the greats of R&B · Bobby "Blue" Bland, Howlin' Wolf, Little Junior Parker, Walter Horton and B. King. Those sides were released by the Chess and RPM labels, and then in 2, Philips established his own Sun Records in Memphis. He was to forever ·luence rock (and country music) by recording Presley, Carl Perkins, Bill Justis, ıarlie Rich, Johnny Cash, Jerry Lee Lewis and Roy Orbison.

CARL PERKINS, ONE OF THE MAINSTAYS OF SUN RECORDS.

HE KING

Elvis Presley was raised in Memphis. For his 11th birthday, he wanted a bicycle — he t a guitar. The guitar became his constant companion. He wasn't terribly noticeable in ɟh school, although his longish black hair (dyed from auburn) with very long sideburns ıs more radical than most. (Later on, he added to this with outrageous clothing.) ·wever, he did discover that when he sang and played in a couple of school talent ɔws he received a lot more attention. After high school, he worked as truck driver, ıyed some local clubs and hung around the clubs where the bluesmen played, ɔecially Junior Parker and Arthur Crudup.

Presley took advantage of Philips' recording service to cut some recordings as gifts his mother ("My Happiness," an old standard ballad), and then went back in early to see if Philips would be interested in him for Sun Records. Philips had him cut ·eral sides, mostly ballads, which didn't create a stir, but he put Presley together with ɔtty Moore, an incredible ·tarist, who worked with him for ·nths on songs in every ıceivable style.

'hilips had said over and over, could find a white man who d the Negro sound and the ɟgro feel, I could make a billion ·ars." And that probably was ıt he had in mind when he ·ed Presley and said, "You want ıake some blues?" According to : legend, Presley ran the 15 :ks to the studio and talked ·ut all the Crudup tunes he knew. / settled on "That's All Right, ·na." The actual recording of the tune came during a break in a rehearsal session, ·n Presley started goofing around and the band joined him. Philips was knocked out in ·ecording booth by what he heard. He quickly had everyone back up to play it again again) and taped it.

ıe dub (copy of the master) was sent to Memphis' premier DJ, Dewey Philips (no ·ion), who played it 30 times in one night. By the time the record was released

SONGWRITERS MIKE STOLLER AND JERRY LEIBER WITH ELVIS IN 1957.

commercially, there was a back order of 5000 copies. Presley then began touring, appeared at the Grand Ole Opry and the Louisiana Hayride and by the end of the year was named eighth Most Promising Hillbilly (!) Artist by *Billboard Magazine* (the music business "bible").

Wherever he went, people didn't know what to make of him. For some he was too country, for some too black. He brought these elements together to create the prototype rock band. And for a burgeoning group of loyal fans he put on quite a show giving it everything he had with wild abandon — from the legendary hip shaking splits to getting down on the stage inches from outreached hands with that customary crooked-lipped guise. The ten cuts he did for Sun had blues and country tinges, but were clean sounding fresh and energetic. These were hits that brought him the "Most Promising C&W Artist" award from Billboard at the end of 1955.

In 1955, seminal country artist manager and booking agent Colonel Tom Parker entered the picture. He managed to sign Presley to exclusive representation, and then bought out his contract with Sun and signed him to RCA. In January 1956, Presley recorded "Heartbreak Hotel" at RCA's Nashville studios. This was his first million seller and what followed for two more yea were 14 consecutive million sellers of man differing styles. Presley's success was uniq in pop music, for he simultaneously toppe the pop, country and R&B charts several times — a feat that many artists continuou strive for now in a time of much looser musical categorization. His influence on rock music and the continuing popularity his music are the reasons he'll always be called "The King."

PRESLEY IN LEATHER – STYLIZED AND SEXIER (PHOTO COURTESY OF RCA RECORDS).

ROCKABILLY

The sound at Sun Records was labeled "Rockabilly." It started with the Sun artists, continued with Ricky Nelson courtesy of h guitarist (James Burton, formerly with Presl through to the Stray Cats and beyond. It was, in Carl Perkins' words, "blues with a country beat," and definitely became whi Southern music. There was an expression going around Memphis at the time — "cat" clothes, "cat" music — from white kids picking up black styles of music and dress. It w there that this form of rebelliousness gave forth to rockabilly — a fusion of the rock an hillbilly sounds. It was embellished by Presley's guitarist Scotty Moore and by the energetic playing/pounding of Jerry Lee Lewis' piano and by the clear, clean sound Buddy Holly. It wasn't a fat or layered sound; you could hear all the chord changes, "decipher" all of the instruments and most of the lyric. One of its sounds — the echo was created by Philips using sewer pipes and singing-in-the-shower acoustics (don't w all sound better there?).

WHOLE LOTTA SHAKIN'...

Presley was the influence on most of these rockabilly artists. Carl Perkins heard Presley's first recording in Jackson, Tennesee, and headed for Sun where he recorde first smash "Blue Suede Shoes." It's said that another Presley fan, Jerry Lee Lewis, camped out on Sun's doorstep and, when not able to corner Philips, got to his assist Jack Clement, and played everything from country to blues to Christmas tunes. Whe

hilips heard the audition tapes he was
ıpressed, told Lewis to learn some rock
' roll, and recorded "Crazy Arms"
hich was a minor success. The
ıbsequent recording session sounds like
reprise of a Presley story: after the
escribed songs were put down, Philips
ld Lewis and his group to play anything
ey wanted. They launched into "Whole
tta Shakin' Goin' On" in one take, and
hit the pop charts and sold a million in
957, making Lewis a rock superstar.
wis made his mark as one of the most
ergetic, uptempo keyboard rockers of
time.

BUDDY HOLLY (PHOTO COURTESY OF MPL COMMUNI-CATIONS)

FOUND MY THRILL...

Another piano man, but from the R&B charts, Fats Domino cut an early million seller hit, "Fat Man," 1953. The recording was a production set up by Dave Bartholomew, a musician and A&R (artist d repertoire) man for L.A.-based Imperial Records. Domino's piano playing was pure New Orleans es, most likely inspired by Professor Longhair, and in that first session Bartholomew brought together group of musicians, arrangers, writers and technical hands (including engineer Cosimo Matassa) t were to stay with Domino continually throughout his other hits. (Domino also played on Lloyd ce's noteworth 1952 crossover hit, "Lawdy Miss Clawdy" (later a Beatles recording).

Domino's sound was mellower than many of the blues singers of the day; there was a smooth-s, a charm to his sound. In 1957, "Blueberry Hill," an old standard, became Domino's biggest Its piano part with its characteristic triplets was the quintessential keyboard sound for many rock lads that followed.

WOP BOP A LOO BOP – A WOP BAM BOOM

Everyone knows that intro to Little Richard's first major hit "Tutti Frutti" — it served notice to the world ın incredible, outrageous showman. Richard Penniman was almost too pretty, with a high shiny npador, a thin, penciled-looking moustache and loads of showy jewelry. He started singing in rch, but at 13 was more attracted to the traveling Southern medicine circuses and periodically ran ay from home. Whenever he was home, he was too weird for his parents who booted him out.

enniman moved in the owners of the Tock Club in con, Georgia, who care of him, got back in school and him perform in club. (The "Little" ichard's name e from displaying alent early.) By 16 vas recording blues CA, followed by a singing doo-wop ored rhythm and s for Peacock rds. Then came and roll...

LITTLE RICHARD IN ACTION. (PHOTO COURTESY OF SPECIALTY RECORDS)

LITTLE RICHARD – CONSUMMATE SHOWMAN. (PHOTO COURTESY OF JESSE LEE, CURRENTLY OF THE COASTERS)

Early in 1955 nothing was happening for Penniman. He did send a demo to Specialty Records and washed dishes at a Greyhound bus station while waiting seven months to hear from them. Art Rupe, the head of Specialty, was sharp enough to book the be of New Orleans' sidemen for a session at th famous J&M Studios of Cosimo Matassa anc on September 14, 1955, "Tutti Frutti" was recorded amongst a group of otherwise forgettable tunes.

"Tutti Frutti" was exciting and "clean" enough to be played on white stations, and Little Richard had an instant rise to stardom. He followed with more hits, "Long Tall Sally," "Rip It Up," "Good Golly Miss Molly," "Slippin' and Slidin'," "Keep A-Knockin'" and "Lucille," and made three movies that showed three very distinct sides of him.

Then,within a short time, at the peak of his popularity in 1957, he made a deal with God. The jewelry was flung into the ocean and he abruptly returned to gospel music and enrolled in bible college. Much later he returned to rock and roll, proclaiming himself as its king. The Beatles had helped keep his sound alive with their version of "Tutti Frutti." And now no rock ar roll hall of fame can be complete unless Little Richard is there.

LLOYD PRICE AND HIS FATHER. NOTE THE FABULOUS TAILORING ON THE JACKET. (PHOTO COURTESY OF SPECIALTY RECORDS)

NEW ORLEANS – DO YOU KNOW WHAT IT MEANS

New Orleans was fertile ground for early rock and roll. As note with Little Richard, Art Rupe of Specialty Records had a knack for finding the New Orleans talent. Predating "Miss Molly" and "Skin Sally," Lloyd Price had an early R&B crossover hit with "Lawdy Mi Clawdy" on Specialty which incorporated typical New Orleans instrumental mixes with his exhuberant vocals. Later his hits includ the Southern classic "Stagger Lee" and the huge smash "(You've Got) Personality." Another Specialty find was Larry Williams who recorded "Bony Maronie" and "Dizzy Miss Lizzie," notable for Williams great vocals, a memorable guitar riff and a groove that was "rough, tough and tore up."

Shirley (Goodman) and (Leonard) Lee, the "Sweethearts Of T Blues," were found doo-wopping on the Latin Quarter street corners by Eddie Mesner of Aladdin Records. Shirley's unusual voice, which hit grace notes with each note she sang, was especially catchy on their biggest hit "Let The Good Times Roll," another tune that became a much-recorded rock standard.

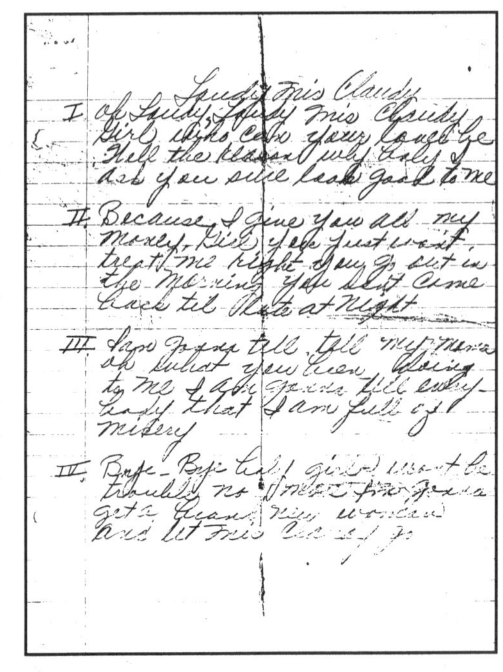

Lawdy Mis Claudy

I. Oh Lawdy, Lawdy Mis Claudy
Girl who can your laugh be
Tell the reason why Only I
Ask you sure look good to me

II. Because I give you all my
Money, Girl you just won't
treat me right You go out in
the morning you don't come
back til late at Night

III. I'm gonna tell, tell my mama
oh what you been doing
to me I am gonna tell everybody that I am full of
misery

IV. Bye-Bye baby girl I won't be
troubled no more I'm gonna
get a clean nice woman
and let Mis Claudy go

A COPY OF A COPY OF LLOYD PRICE'S HAND-WRITTEN MANUSCRIPT FOR *LAWDY MIS CLAUDY* (SIC). (COURTESY OF SPECIALTY RECORDS)

DOO WOP – SWEET AS HONEY FRO THE VINE

It started with sweet rhythm and blues ballads. During the b of rock and roll, doo wop was the transitional phase, the ultim in crossover on the charts between black and white.

The doo wop groups achieved the apex of vocal harmony often sang almost a cappella. The name comes from the nons syllables the background singers sang behind the leader, eith very low or very high — sometimes as a sort of vocal rhythm strument, at times just to accent or punctuate the chord changes.

The Penguins' "Earth Angel" is considered to be one of the premiere &B classics. The group, named after the Kool Cigarette trademark, ere still students at L.A.'s Fremont High School when Dootsie Williams, ocal record producer and owner of Dootone Records, signed them. arth Angel" was on the B side of a recording that bombed, but when record was flipped, everyone went nuts over the sweetness of the e. It hit number one on the R&B charts, and eight on the pop charts, then had to battle with a cover recording by a white group, the ew-Cuts (known for covering "Sh-Boom").

White groups covering black tunes was common with many of the ngs. This was a trend that DJ Alan Freed courageously fought ainst by playing the original black recordings and always giving dit to rock's roots in R&B. The Diamonds were one group especially own for its covers of other recordings. One of their many doo wop covers was "Silhouettes," a story song with a twist, and a pure rock tune, ack Denim Trousers."

When music manager Buck Ram took over managing the Penguins he gotiated a deal with Mercury Records that included them and his then nown group, the Platters. As with most of the doo wop groups, the Penguins d only one hit, but the Platters, on the other hand, were wildly successful (see *tory Of Rock – The Late 50s*). Their lead singer, tenor Tony Williams, had a ce as smooth as silk, and Ram had a record promotion person, Jeannie nett, who hounded radio stations relentlessly. After a year of promo, "Only (And You Alone)" finally broke in Seattle, went on to number 5 on the onal charts and stayed on the charts for 28 weeks!

LARRY WILLIAMS CONTEMPLATING THE FAME OF HIS FAVORITE GIRLS, BONY MORONIE AND DIZZY MISS LIZZY. (PHOTO COURTESY OF SPECIALTY RECORDS)

AN EXAMPLE OF AN UNUSUAL "COVER" RECORD: PAT BOONE COVERING *TUTTI FRUTTI* WHICH CHARTED HIGHER THAN LITTLE RICHARD'S ORIGINAL VERSION. (SHEET MUSIC COURTESY OF THE COLLECTION OF RONNY S. SCHIFF)

HE GUITAR

s Link Wray made guitar instrumental inroads on the recording of cket '88" (and his later recording of "Rumble"), the guitar as a standout instrument came into its own around 1957. Sun Records producer and io musician, Bill Justis experimented with an exaggerated echo and a ved-down vibrato on his electric guitar. He produced the wailing umental "Raunchy" (which is also known for its memorable rough, funknted tenor sax solo). Guitarists such as Wray were beginning to use ortion, Duane Eddy was using a highly amplified Fender bass played like itar and another new invention — the electric tremolo.

remost among record companies who found and promoted performers great guitar chops was ss Records, headed by ard Chess, in Chicago. At ecommendation of the ous bluesman Muddy ers, they recorded the most rtant guitar influence of the Chuck Berry. Berry hit high e R&B charts in the '50s, enerally wasn't making it to op charts. It would be a before his style, techniques licks would filter through, hen they did, it was his ence on guitar that was the

THE FONTANE SISTERS

THE PLATTERS SINGING SWEETLY IN THE MOTION PICTURE *ROCK ALL NIGHT*. (PHOTO COURTESY OF A.M.C., INC.)

strongest. And you'll find lists of guitarists and groups — Clapton, the Stones, etc. — that cite him as their major influence. (See *History Of Rock*, Volume 3.)

CHUCK BERRY, VERY YOUNG AND VERY POISED.

Chess scored with another guitarist, Bo Diddley, who was also influenced by Muddy Waters. His first hit was the blues-tinged "I'm A Man," his second was his eponymous "Bo Diddley," known for its od "jungle beat" and the rhythmic Diddley signature of "shave-and-a-haircut-two-bits." Where Berry was known for his techniques and licks Diddley was known for his rhythmic style. In the mid-'50s, he was als a forerunner in the use of electric guitar with *two* Fender bassman am with extra speakers, plus he used a lot of echo and a tremolo unit tha he invented. Diddley's sound and style influenced Presley and Buddy Holly; his use of electronics was to lay the groundwork for Jimi Hendr and generations of heavy metal guitarists.*

ROCK AND ROLL IS HERE TO STAY

By 1955, the teenage world had embraced rock as their languag As *Rebel Without A Cause* became a symbol of teen rebellion, rock and roll picked up the anthem. "Black Denim Trousers" was one suc tune that embodied the image of the "tough," and to this day the uniform hasn't changed significantly — "He wore black denim trousers and motorcycle boots and a black leather jacket with an eagle on the back." The tune also brought tw young California songwriters, Jerry Leiber and Mike Stoller, to national fame.

Leiber was influenced by country music and blues from his native Baltimore, and th by the blues coming out of record companies like Specialty Reco when he moved to L.A. Stoller's influences came from black musi heard in Harlem when he lived in New York and them from his heavily Latino home turf in L.A. Six months after they started as a team, Leiber and Stoller had their first hit. While writing and producing for Federal Records in the mid-'50s they penned some Big Mama Thornton R&B hits including "Hound Dog" and "Kans City." These were later to become giant hits with Presley, who recorded a countless number of their tunes. They also were the fi producers to sign an independent production deal with a record company (a landmark, since this took power from company executives and moved it outside to independent producers).

BO DIDDLEY AND HIS UNIQUE GUITAR.

Another writer who penned many of Presley's hits was Brookly born Otis Blackwell, who wrote "All Shook Up" and "Don't Be Cruel" (plus "Return To Sender" and "Paralyzed"). Blackwell als had a terrific voice and cut many of his own demos, usually with well-known musicians of the day. These excellent demos then set guide to other artists' final recordings, as in Presley's "Teddy Bec Blackwell's diversity can be seen in his two Jerry Lee Lewis hits "Great Balls Of Fire" "Breathless." He had a knack for the rock and roll experience — understanding the feelings and hang-ups of teens and putting these into his songs.

By 1957, what Alan Freed set into motion was further enhanced to major proportio the nationwide, five-days-a-week airing of Dick Clark's *American Bandstand*. Through C and the *Bandstand*, rock and roll entered its next phase.

*Fred Sokolow, *Bo Diddley Guitar Solos*. Hal Leonard Publishing Corp.

ROCK & ROLL GLOSSARY

rtists and repertoire: The cord company personnel responsible r talent acquisition, overseeing their oduction (and repertoire) and their tivities.

x: A musical instrument.

rill Building: Located at 1619 oadway in New York City. Home of ndreds of music publishers' offices. any, many hits were born there.

&W: Country and western music.

art: A sequential list of hits; a itten down musical arrangement provised arrangement is called a ad arrangement).

ops: A musician's playing hnique, ability.

ol: In the '50s, to be hip, in style, y.

ver: A new recording of a viously recorded song. A common ctice in the '50s was for white sts to cover hits by black R&B artists.

ossover: Songs that "cross r" from one chart to another, such rom a country chart to a pop chart.

: n. A record; or one song on an m. **v.** To make (cut) a recording.

mo: A demonstration record; by songwriters and publishers to heir songs to artists.

tortion devices: For guitar ah-wah pedal, fuzz tone, reverb, , tremolo.

o wop: A type of close ony singing, usually with sparse umental accompaniment, unique in se of nonsense syllables as mic background or "punctuation."

dub: n. A copy of the master. **v.** To record from a *master*; to insert a new sound, or synchronize one sound with another sound (overdub).

feedback: On a guitar set for feedback, a string will vibrate at a certain pitch so that the sound is picked up by the amplifier and fed back into the string to increase its vibration at that pitch.

funk: A rhythm and blues sound, usually lowdown, rhythmic and rough.

fuzztone: A device on a guitar that changes the shape of the soundwave so that the music from the amplifier has a blurred or fuzzy sound. First used by Link Wray.

groove: n. Where music really "clicks" and comes together for the listener, especially rhythmically; as in "in the groove." **v.** To *groove* is to enjoy, be one with (the music or one's lover). **adj.** *Groovy*, in the late '60s/early '70s — anything pleasurable or good.

hook: A repetitive phrase, usually in the chorus, that catches the listener's attention.

jive: n. Slang or colloquial expressions derived from blues slang, used first in the jazz sector and then in '50s rock. **v.** In the early '70s, "don't jive me" meant "don't put me on."

master: n. Final, complete recording from which copies can be made. **v.** To master; to make a master.

mix: To balance all the tracks of a multitrack master to bring it to final product status.

overdub: To add parts to and synchronize them in a multitrack recording.

R&B: *Rhythm and blues;* post World War II black music, replacing the previous appellation of "race music."

reverb: On a guitar, an echo-like sound effect.

riff: A pattern of music, sometimes repetitive; usually played by a rhythm instrument — guitar, bass, drum or keyboards.

square: Unhip, uncool, conservative, unknowing in the ways of rock and roll; usually pertaining to one's parents.

standard: A song that continues to remain popular and receive many *covers* over the years.

studio musician: A free-lance musician who works primarily in recording studios.

wah-wah pedal: On guitar, a device that distorts the sound by use of electric currents that vibrate the speakers to emphasize or de-emphasize the middle range of the sound output.

ROCKET '88

Copyright © 1951 by Unichappell Music, Inc.
Copyright Renewed
International Copyright Secured All Rights Reserved
Unauthorized copying, arranging, adapting, recording or public performance is an infringement of copyright.
Infringers ar liable under the law.

heard of ja - lop - ies. You've heard the noise they make. But let me
Instrumental
Instrumental
in - tro - duce my new Rock - et Eight - y Eight. Yes,
G7
D
it's straight. Just one way.
Ev-'ry-bod-y likes my
Rock-et Eight-y Eight. Ba-by, we'll ride in style.
G7
Mov - in' all a-long.

D
To Coda
V - Eight mo - tor, 'n' its mo - dern de - sign. Black con -
ver - ti - ble top _ and the gals _ don't mind.
G7
Spor - tin' with me, _ rid - in'
D
D.S. al Co
all 'round town for joy.
Blow your horn, Raymond. Blow it!

CODA
Step in my Rock - et and don't be late. Ba - by we're
pull - ing out a - bout half past eight.
G7
Go - in' 'round the cor - ner and
D
get a fifth. Ev - 'ry - bod - y in my car's gon - na take a lit - tle nip.
A7
G7
D
Move on out ooz - ing and cruis - ing a - long.

G7
D
G
A7
D

LAWDY MISS CLAWDY

Copyright © 1952 VENICE MUSIC
Copyright Renewed
All Rights Controlled and Administered by EMI BLACKWOOD MUSIC INC. under license from ATV MUSIC (VENICE)
All Rights Reserved International Copyright Secured Used by Permission

2
F
Bb Cb C Bb
F
C7
Guitar Tacet
Oh bye, bye,
F7
Bb
Guitar Tacet
Bb7
ba - by,
Girl! I won't be bad no more
F
Bb
Gm7
C7
Good - bye my Claw - dy down the road I go

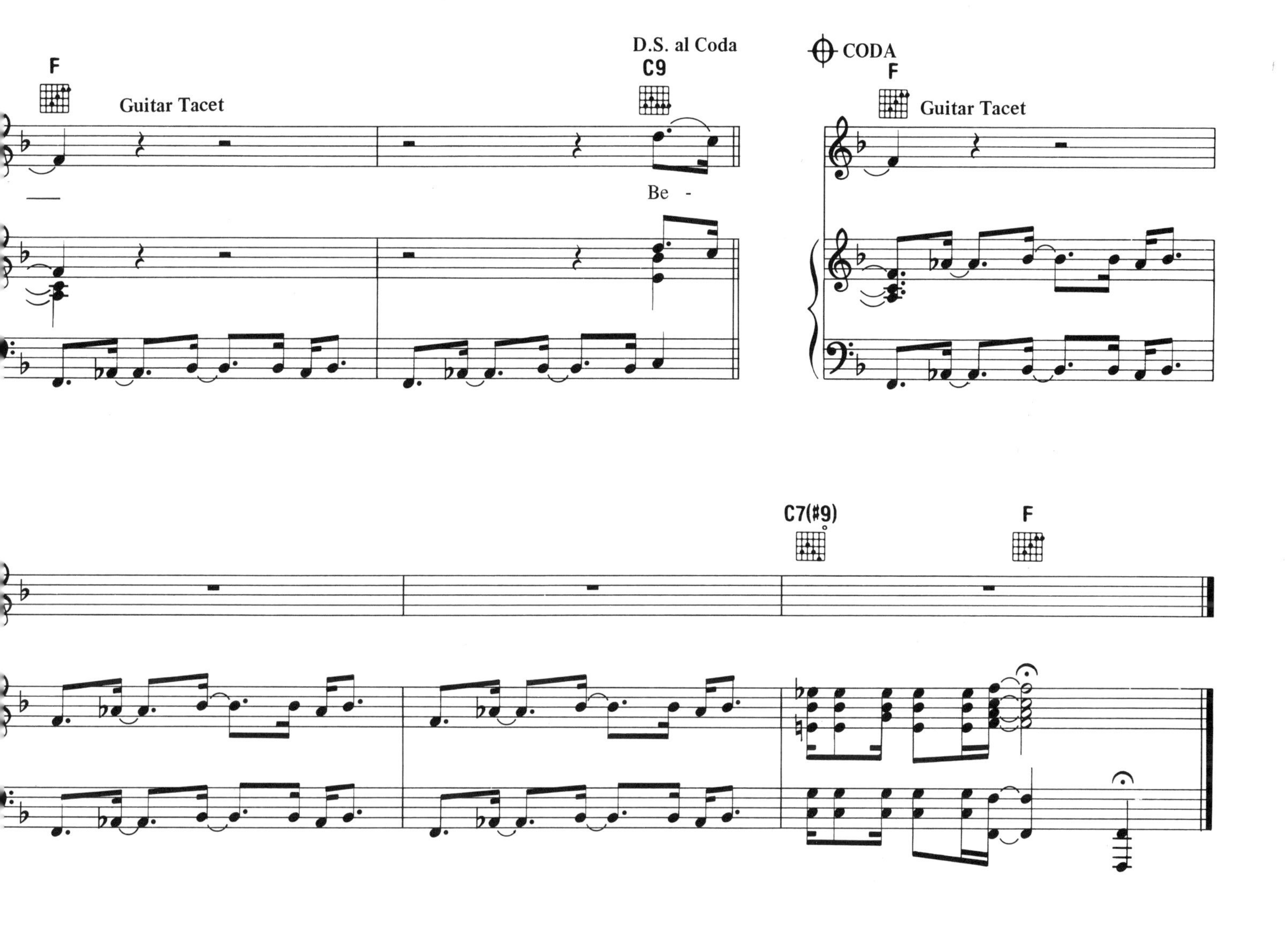

ADDITIONAL VERSES

I'm gonna tell, tell my Mama
Lawd I'm gonna tell her what you been doing to me
I'm gonna tell ev'rybody that I'm down in misery.
Well now Lawdy, Lawdy, Lawdy Miss Clawdy
Girl! You sure look good to me
You just wheeling and rocking baby
You're just as fine as you can be.

SH-BOOM
(Life Could Be A Dream)

Words and Music by JAMES KEYES, CLAUDE FEASTER, CARL FEASTER, FLOYD McRAE and JAMES EDWARDS

Copyright © 1954 by Hill & Range Songs, Inc.
Copyright Renewed
All Rights controlled by Unichappell Music, Inc. (Rightsong Music, Publisher)
International Copyright Secured All Rights Reserved
Unauthorized copying, arranging, adapting, recording or public performance is an infringement of copyright.
Infringers are liable under the law.

Fm7 Bb7 Eb Cm Fm7 Bb7
boom. If you would tell me I'm the on - ly one that you love, life could be a dream, sweet-
Eb Cm Fm7 Bb7 Eb Cm
heart. Hel-lo, hel-lo a - gain, sh - boom, and hop - in' we'll meet a - gain. Oh, life could be a dream, sh -
Fm Bb7 Eb Cm Fm7 Bb7
boom, if on - ly all my pre - cious plans would come true, sh - boom. If you would let me spend my
Eb Cm Fm7 Bb7 Eb Ab7 Eb Ab7
whole life lov - in' you, life could be a dream, sweet - heart.

G7
C7
Ev - 'ry time I look at you___ some - thing is on my mind.___
F7
Fm7
Bb7
If you'd do what I want you to,___ ba - by, we'd be so fine.___ Oh,
Eb
Cm
Fm7
Bb7
Eb
Cm
life could be a dream,___ sh - boom, if I could take you up in Par - a - dise up a - bove, sh -
Fm7
Bb7
Eb
Cm
Fm7
Bb7
To Coda
boom. If you would tell me I'm the on - ly one that you love, life could be a dream, swee

Eb Cm Fm7 Bb7
heart.
Sh -
boom sh - boom, ya da da da da da da da da da. Sh - boom sh - boom, ya da da da da da da da da da. Sh-
Guitar Tacet
boom sh - boom, ya da da da da da da da da da, sh - boom.
D.S. al Coda
CODA
boom.
heart.

GOODNIGHT, IT'S TIME TO GO

(aka GOODNIGHT, SWEETHEART, GOODNIGHT)

Words and Music by JAMES HUDSON
and CALVIN CARTER

Copyright © 1953 & 1954 (Renewed) Arc Music Corp.
All Rights Reserved

C Cm G Am7 D7 G G7 C Cm
real-ly must say,— GOOD - NIGHT, sweet heart, good-night.
1. Well, it's three - o'- clock in the
2. Now, my moth - er — and my
G G7 C G Am7 G G7 C Cm
morn - ing, Ba - by, — I just can't treat you right, Well, I hate to leave you, ba - by, —
fa - ther, Might hear if I stay here too — long, One — kiss — and we'll part, — And
G F9 E7 A7 D7 G Em
Don't mean may - be, be - cause — I — love — you so.
you'll be go - ing, you know I hate to see — you go.
Good - night, sweet-heart, well, it's
Am7 D7 G Em Am7 D7 G G7
time to go, — Good-night, sweet-heart, well, it's time to go, — I hate to leave you, but I
C Cm G Am7 D7 1. G6 E C7-9 D9 2. G6 A♭6 G6
real-ly must say, — GOOD - NIGHT, sweet-heart, good - night. NIGHT.
3 3 3 3 3 3 3 3

SHAKE, RATTLE AND ROLL

Words and Music by
CHARLES CALHOUN

Moderately Bright
mf

VERSE
C6
Get out ___ from that kitch - en and rat - tle those pots and pans, ___

C7
F9
C6
Get out ___ from that kitch - en and rat - tle those pots and pans. ___

Copyright © 1954 by Progressive Music Publishing Co., Inc.
Copyright Renewed
All rights controlled by Unichappell Music, Inc. (Rightsong Music, Publisher)
International Copyright Secured All Rights Reserved
Unauthorized copying, arranging, adapting, recording or public performance is an infringement of copyright.
Infringers are liable under the law.

Cdim
Dm7
G9
C6
Well, roll my breakfast, 'cause I'm a hungry man.
CHORUS
C6
Shake Rat-tle and Roll,
Shake rat-tle and roll,
C7
F9
Shake rat-tle and roll,
C6
Shake rat-tle and roll;
Cdim
Dm7
G7
You nev-er do noth-in' to save your dog-gone

1
C6
to 2nd Verse
soul.
2
C6
to 3rd Verse
soul.
3
C6
Fine
soul.
Verse 2
C6
Wear - in' those dress - es, your hair done up so righ
C7
F9
Wear - in' those dress - es, your
C6
hair done up so right;
Cdim
You

Dm7
G9
C6
D.S. 2nd ending
look so warm, but your heart is cold as ice.
Verse 3
C6
I'm like a one-eyed cat, peep-in' in a sea-food store,
C7
F9
I'm like a one-eyed cat,
C6
Cdim
Dm7
peep-in' in a sea-food store; I can look at you, tell you

C7
C6
Verse 4
C6
don't love me no more.
I be-
lieve you're do-in' me wrong and now I know,
C7
I be-
F9
C6
Cdim
lieve you're do-in' me wrong and now I know;
The
Dm7
G7
C6
D.S. al Fine
(3rd ending)
more I work, the fast-er my mon-ey goes.

EARTH ANGEL

© Copyright 1954 by Dootsie Williams Publications
© Copyright Renewal 1982 by Dootsie Williams Publications
International Copyright Secured All Rights Reserved

Fm7
Bb7
Eb
Cm
Fm7
Bb7
The one I a - dore,
Love you for - ev - er and ev - er - more.
Eb
Cm
Fm7
Bb7
Eb
Ab
Eb
Fm7
I'm just a fool,
A fool in love with you.
Eb7
Ab
Abm
Eb
I fell for you,
And I knew the
Fm7
Bb7
Eb
Eb7
Ab
Cdim
vi - sion of your love's love - li - ness,
I hope and I pray

Eb Cm F9 B7 Bb7
That some day I'll be the vi - sion of your hap - pi - ness. Earth
Eb Cm Fm7 Bb7 Eb Cm
an - gel, earth an - gel, Please be mine, My dar - ling, dear,
Fm7 Bb7 Eb Cm Fm7 Bb7
Love you all the time. I'm just a fool, A fool in love with
1 Eb Cdim Fm7 Bb7 2 Eb Fm7 Eb
you. Earth you.

TWEEDLEE DEE

Words and Music by
WINFIELD SCOTT

Copyright © 1954 Unichappell Music, Inc. (Rightsong Music Publisher)
Copyright Renewed
International Copyright Secured All Rights Reserved
Unauthorized copying, arranging, adapting, recording or public performance is an infringement of copyright.
Infringers are liable under the law.

F C+ F7 Bb7
Jim - i - ny Crick - ets, Jim - i - ny Jack, You make my heart go click - i - ty clack,
Hunk - ies, hunk - ies, piec - es, bite, I'm gon - na see my hon - ey to - night,
F Bb9 F F+ F6 F F+ F6
Tweed - lee, tweed - lee, tweed - lee dee.
Tweed - lee, tweed - lee, tweed - lee dot.
Bb F
Tweed - lee dee, tweed - le dee dee,
Tweed - lee do, tweed - le dee do
mp-mf
Bb F
Give it up, give it up, give your love to me.
Give that kiss to me be - fore you go;

Bb
F
Tweed - lee dot, tweed-le dee dot,
Tweed - lee dum, tweed-le dee dum,
C7
D7
G7
C7
Gim-me, gim-me, gim-me, gim-me, give me all the love you got.
Look-ie, look-ie, look-ie, look-ie, look at that sug - ar plum.
F
Bb9
Hum - ty, um - bum bum Tweed - lee, tweed - lee, tweed - lee do, dum,
F
F+
F6
F
F+
F6
F
I'm a
You're as

F#dim
Gm
Eb6
C7
Gm
Eb6
C7
luck - y so and so;
sweet as bub - ble gum;
F
C+
F7
Bb7
Hub - ba, hub - ba, hon - ey, do,
Mer - cy, mer - cy pud - din' pie,
I'm gon - na keep my
You've got some - thin' that
F
Bb9
eyes on you,
mon - ey can't buy,
Tweed - lee, tweed - lee, tweed - lee do.
dum.
1
F
F+
F6
F
F+
F6
2
F
F+
F6
F
F+
F6
sf

I'M A MAN

Words and Music by
ELLAS McDANIEL

Copyright © 1955 (Renewed 1965) by Arc Music Corp.
International Copyright Secured All Rights Reserved

G C G C G C
I spell M A N
G C G C G C
Man. The line I shoot
G C G C
will nev - er miss, The way I make love to 'em
G C G C G C
they can't re - sist, Now I'm a man I spell M

G
C
G
C
G
C
A
N
Man.
G
C
G
Gmaj7
G7
G
Gmaj7
G7
G7
C
G
C
G
C
Go - in' back down
G
C
G
C
to Kan - sas to
bring back a lit - tle girl

G
C
G
C
G
C
just like you.
Now I'm a man
I spell M
A
N
Man.
F
F#

ROCK AROUND THE CLOCK

By MAX C. FREEDMAN
and JIMMY DeKNIGHT

Copyright © 1953 by Myers Music, Inc.
Copyright Renewed
International Copyright Secured All Rights Reserved

F7
B♭9
clock strikes one, We're gon-na rock a-round the clock to-night, We're gon-na
yell for more, We're gon-na rock a-round the clock to-night, We're gon-na
sev-enth heav'n, We're gon-na rock a-round the clock to-night, We're gon-na
so will you, We're gon-na rock a-round the clock to-night, We're gon-na
clock a-gain, We're gon-na rock a-round the clock to-night, We're gon-na
F
G7
rock, rock, rock, 'til broad day-light, We're gon-na rock, gon-na rock a-round
Gm7
C7♯5
C9sus
1-4
F
the clock to-night.
2. When the
3. When the
4. When it's
5. When the
5
F

BLACK DENIM TROUSERS AND MOTORCYCLE BOOTS

Words and Music by JERRY LEIBER and MIKE STOLLER

© 1955 Jerry Leiber Music and Mike Stoller Music
Copyright Renewed
All Rights Administered by WB Music Corp.
All Rights Reserved Used by Permission

G7
had a hopped - up cy - cle that took off like a gun. That
Cm
fool was the ter - ror of high - way 1 0 1.
Cm6/9
Cm(maj9)
Cm
Well, he nev - er washed his face and he
Lou, poor girl, she plead-ed and she
G7
nev - er combed his hair. He had ax - le grease em - bed - ded un - der
begged him not to leave. She said, "I've got a feel - ing if you

Cm
neath his fin - ger - nails. On the mus - cle of his arm was a
ride to - night I"ll grieve." But her tears were shed in vain, and her
Fm
G7
red tat - too, a pic - ture of a heart say - ing,
ev - 'ry word was lost in the rum - ble of his en - gine and the
Cm
"Moth - er I love you." He had a pret - ty girl - friend by the
smoke from his ex - haust. He took off like a dev - il, there was
G7
name of Ma - ry Lou, but he treat - ed her just like he
fi - re in his eyes. He said, "I'll go a thou - sand miles be -

Cm
treat-ed all __ the rest. And ev - 'ry - bod - y pit-ied her __ 'cause
fore the sun can rise. But he hit a scream - ing die - sel that was
Fm
G7
ev - 'ry - bod - y knew__ he loved that dog-gone mo - tor - cy - cle
Cal - i - for - nia bound, and when they cleared the wreck-age all they
Cm
G7
best. He wore
found. was his
black den - im trou-sers and mo-tor - cy - cle boots and a
Cm
black leath - er jack - et with an ea - gle on the back.
He
But they

G7
had a hopped - up cy - cle that took off like a gun. That
could - n't find the cy - cle that took off like a gun, and they
1
Fm
D♭
Cm
Cm6/9
fool was the ter - ror of high - way 1 0 1.
3
3
3
3

D♭13(♯11)
Cm
Mar - y
2
Fm
G7
Cm
D/C
D♭/C
nev - er found the ter - ror of high - way 1 0 1.
Cm6/9
Cm(maj9)
Cm

ONLY YOU
(And You Alone)

TRO - © Copyright 1955 (renewed 1983) Hollis Music, Inc., New York, NY
International Copyright Secured
All Rights Reserved Including Public Performance For Profit
Used by Permission

D7
B13
B9
Em
lone can thrill me like you do, and
A9
D7sus
D9
D.S. al Coda
fill my heart with love for On - ly You. On - ly
CODA
Cm6
G
E7
un - der - stand the mag - ic that you do. You're my
A9
Eb7
D7
D9
D7-9
G
F9
Gmaj7
dream come true, my one and On - ly You.

BO DIDDLEY

Copyright © 1955 (Renewed) Arc Music Corp.
All Rights Reserved

G
BO DID-DL-EY caught a nan - ny goat,
To make his pret-ty ba-by a
R.H.
Sun-day coat.
BO DID-DL-EY caught a bear - cat,
R.H.
Dm7
G
To make his pret-ty ba-by a Sun-day hat.
Instrumental Interlude
Dm7
G
Dm7
ff
G
(Tacet)
G6
mf

G
G6
G
Won't you come to my house and rack that bone,
Take my ba-by all the
mp
G6
G
way from home.
Look at that bo-do, Oh, where's he been,
G6
G
G6
Up to your house and gone a-gain.
Refrain (Repeat ad lib. gradually fading out)
G
BO DID-DL-EY, BO DID-DL-EY, have you heard,
My
mf
R.H.
pret-ty ba-by said she was a bird.
R.H.

SEE YOU LATER, ALLIGATOR

Words and Music by
ROBERT GUIDRY

© 1955 (Renewed) Arc Music Corp.
All Rights Reserved

C6
with an - oth - er man to - day.
near - ly made me lose my head.
You know my love is just for you.
I know you meant it just for play.
G7
When I asked her what's the mat - ter;
But the next time that I saw her,
Won't you say that you'll for - give me,
Don't you know you real - ly hurt me,
C6
This is what I heard her say.
Re-mind-ed her of what she said.
And say your love for me is true.
And this is what I have to say.
no chord
See you lat - er, al - li -
C6
ga - tor,
af - ter 'while croc - o - dile;

C7
F9
See you lat - er, al - li - ga - tor,
C6
af - ter 'while croc - o - dile,
G7
Can't you see you're in my way, now, don't you know you cramp my
1,2,3
C6
no chord
style?
2. When I thought of what she
3. She said, I'm sor - ry, pret - ty
4. I said, wait a min - ute,
4
C
D♭6
C6
style?

TUTTI FRUTTI

Words and Music by R. PENNIMAN
and D. LA BOSTRIE

Copyright © 1955, Renewed 1983 VENICE MUSIC CORPORATION
All Rights Controlled and Administered by EMI BLACKWOOD MUSIC INC. under the license from ATV MUSIC (VENICE)
International Copyright Secured All Rights Reserved Used by Permission

G7
rut - ti, Tut - ti Frut - ti au rut - ti, Tut - ti
D9
C9
Frut - ti au rut - ti, A -
G Am7 G Am7 G
bop - bop a - loom - op a - lop bop boom! I got a
gal, her name's Sue, She knows just what to do,
gal, her name's Dai - sy, She al - most drives me cra -

G7
C7
I got a gal, her name's Sue, She
zy. I got a gal, her name's Dai - sy, She
G
C7
G
knows just what to do. I've
al - most drives me cra - zy. She's a
been to the east, I've been to the west, But
real gone cook - ie, yes - sir - ree, But
C7
she's the gal I love the best.
pret - ty lit - tle Su - zy's the gal for me.
Tut - ti Frut - ti au

G
rut - ti, Tut - ti Frut - ti au rut - ti, Tut - ti
C7
G
Frut - ti au rut - ti, Tut - ti Frut - ti au
D9
C9
rut - ti, Tut - ti Frut - ti au rut - ti, A -
G
Am7
1
2
bop - bop a - loom - op a - lop bop boom! (2) I got a lop bop boom!

EDDIE MY LOVE

Words and Music by AARON COLLINS,
MAXWELL DAVIS and SAM LING

© 1955 Powerforce Music
Copyright Renewed 1983
International Copyright Secured All Rights Reserved

C
Am
Dm7
G7
C
Am7
Please, Ed - die,
don't make me wait too long.
Dm7
G7
C
Am7
Ed - die please write.
Dm7
G7
C
Am7
me one line.
Tell me your love is
Dm7
C
Am7
still on - ly mine.
Please, Ed - die,

Dm7
G7
C
F
don't make me wait too long.
C
G7
F
C
You left me last Sep-tem-ber to re-
F
C
F
turn to me be-fore long. But all I do is cry
C
Dm7
G7
my-self to sleep, Ed-die, since you've been go-o-one,

C
Am7
Dm7
G7
Ed - die my love,
I'm sink - ing fast,
The ver - y next day
might be my last.
Please, Ed - die,
don't make me wait too long.
F
C7
1
2
You lo - o - ong.

HEARTBREAK HOTEL

By MAE BOREN AXTON, TOMMY DURDEN
and ELVIS PRESLEY

Copyright © 1956 by Tree Publishing Co., Inc., 8 Music Square West, Nashville, TN 37203
Copyright Renewed
This arrangement Copyright © 1984 by Tree Publishing Co., Inc.
International Copyright Secured All Rights Reserved

E
F
though it's al - ways crowd - ed, still can find some room,
Bell - hop's tears keep flow - ing, desk clerks dressed in black,
where those bro - ken heart - ed lov - ers cry a - way their gloom, oh!
They been so long on Lone - ly Street they ain't nev - er gonn' come back, oh!
A7
Bb7
I get so lone - ly I get so lone - ly
3
B7
C7
E
F
D.C. (verse 4) and Fade
get so lone ly I could die.

BLUE SUEDE SHOES

Words and Music by
CARL LEE PERKINS

Bright Tempo (not too fast)

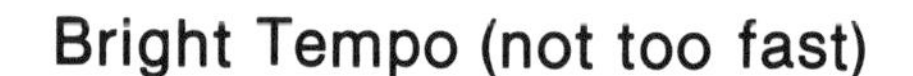

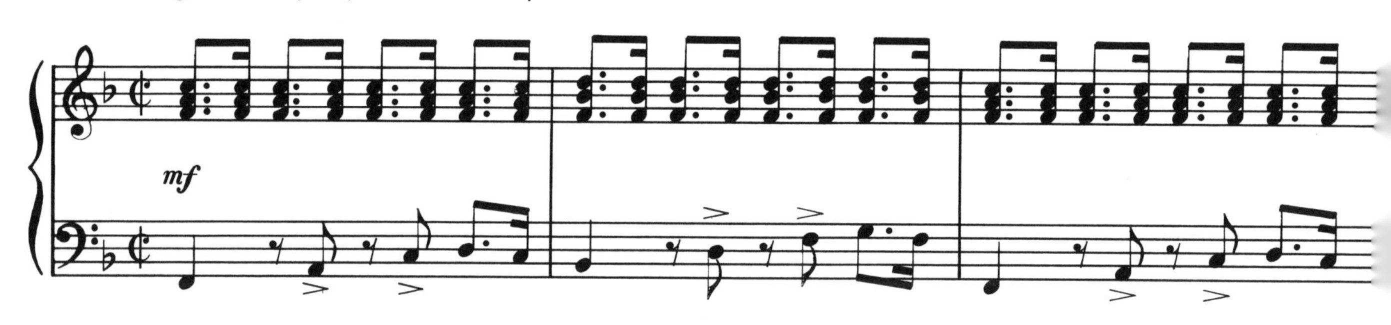
mf

Chorus

C
(tacet)
F7
(tacet)
F7
Well, it's one for the mon - ey, two for the show,
f

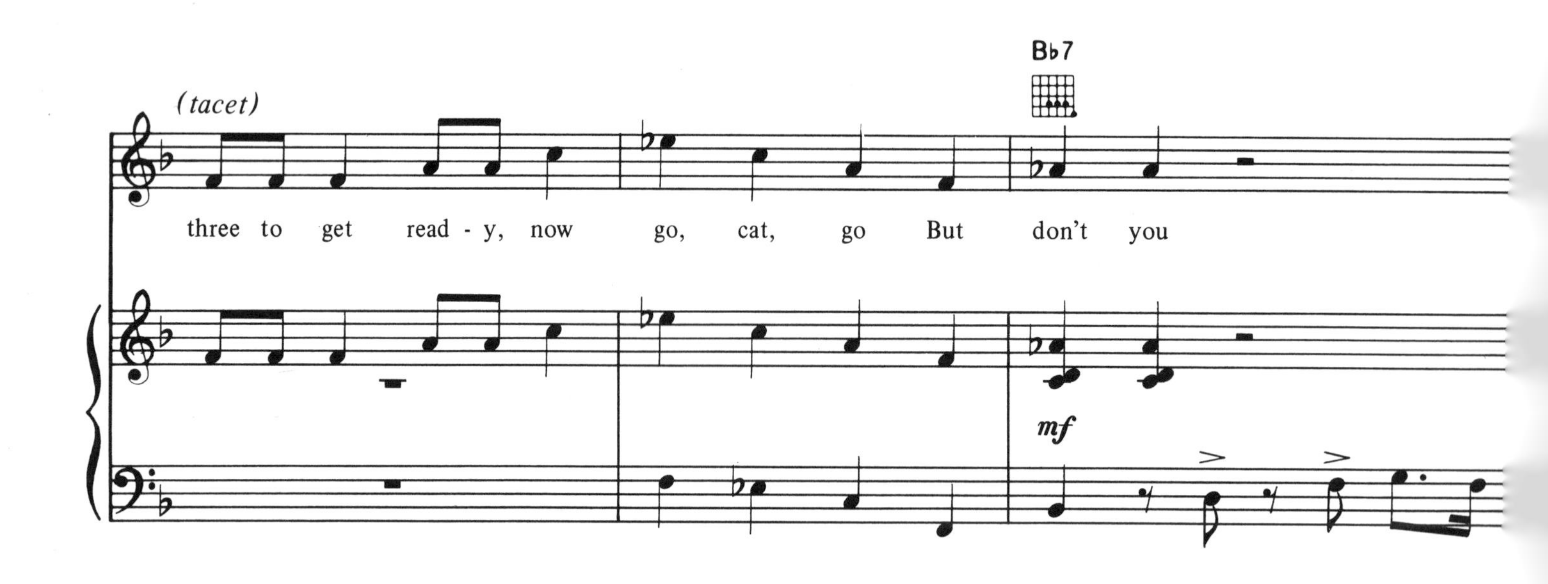
(tacet)
Bb7
three to get read - y, now go, cat, go But don't you
mf

Copyright © 1956 by Hi-Lo Music, Inc.
Copyright Renewed
Controlled in the U.S.A. by Unichappell, Inc. (Published by Rightsong Music, Inc. and Hi-Lo Music, Inc.)
International Copyright Secured All Rights Reserved
Unauthorized copying, arranging, adapting, recording or public performance is an infringement of copyright.
Infringers are liable under the law.

F
step on my Blue Suede Shoes. You can
C
Bb
F
Bb7
do an-y-thing but lay off of my Blue Suede Shoes.
F
C
(tacet)
F7
(tacet)
F7
Well, you can knock me down, step on my face,
Burn my house, steal my car,
f
(tacet)
F7
(tacet)
slan-der my name all o-ver the place;
drink my ci-der from my old fruit jar;
Do an-y-thing that you

F7
Bb7
want to do, but uh - uh, hon - ey, lay off of my shoes Don't you
mf
F
F
step on my Blue Suede Shoes. You can
C
Bb
1 F
Bb7
do an - y - thing but lay off of my Blue Suede Shoes.
F
C
(tacet)
2 F
Bb7
F
F7(#9)
Well, you can Shoes.

LONG TALL SALLY

By ENOTRIS JOHNSON,
RICHARD PENNIMAN and ROBERT BLACKWELL

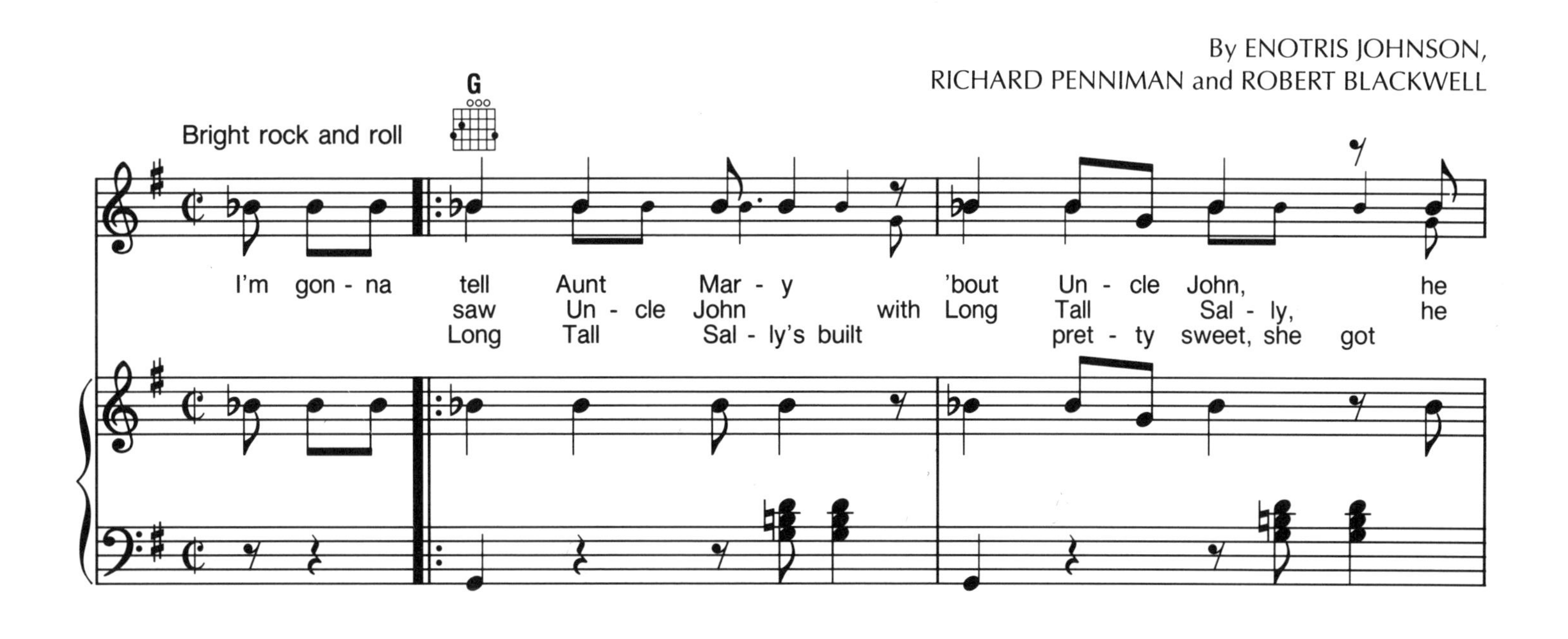
G
Bright rock and roll
I'm gon - na tell Aunt Mar - y 'bout Un - cle John, he
saw Un - cle John with Long Tall Sal - ly, he
Long Tall Sal - ly's built pret - ty sweet, she got

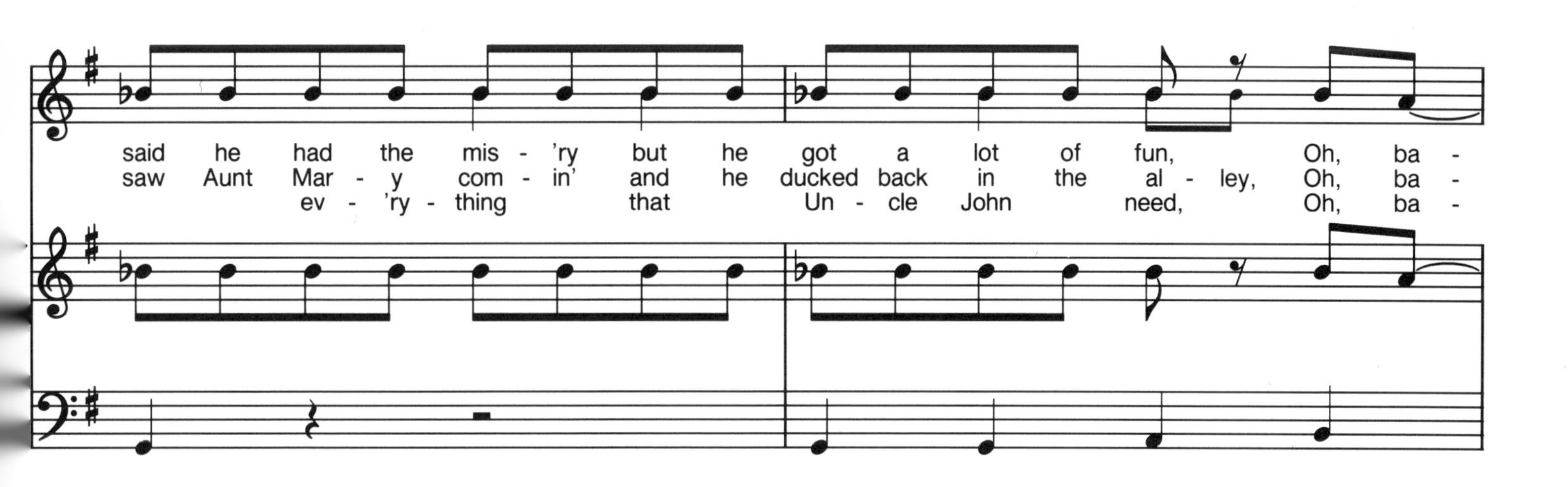
said he had the mis - 'ry but he got a lot of fun, Oh, ba -
saw Aunt Mar - y com - in' and he ducked back in the al - ley, Oh, ba -
ev - 'ry - thing that Un - cle John need, Oh, ba -

C
G
- by,
- by,
- by,
yeah, now ba - by,

Copyright © 1956 VENICE MUSIC CORPORATION
Copyright Renewed
All Rights for the U.S., Canada and Mexico Controlled and Administered by EMI BLACKWOOD MUSIC INC. under license from ATV MUSIC (VENICE)
All Rights Reserved International Copyright Secured Used by Permission

D7
Woo,
ba
-
by,
C7
G
D7
some fun to - night.
I
D7
G7
C7

G7
D7
C7
G7
D7
3
D7
G7
Well
G♯
A
B♭
B

C
G
D7
C7
G
D7
G
Well we're gon - na have some fun to - night,
have some fun to - night,
(oo)

C7
G
Ev - 'ry - thing's all right,
have some fun to - night,
D7
1
C7
Have some fun,
(2nd time) Yeah, we'll have some fun,
yeah, yeah,
G
D7
2
C7
yeah,
(Wow)
We're gon - na
some fun to - night.
G
C
C#dim7
D7
G7
G9

SLIPPIN' AND SLIDIN'

Words and Music by
EDWIN J. BOCAGE, ALBERT COLLINS,
RICHARD PENNIMAN and JAMES SMITH

© 1956 Renewed 1984 VENICE MUSIC, INC. and BESS MUSIC
All Rights for VENICE MUSIC, INC. Controlled and Administered by EMI BLACKWOOD MUSIC INC. under license from ATV MUSIC (VENICE).
All Rights Reserved International Copyright Secured Used by Permission

F7
go. ___ Slip - pin' and a - slid - in', peep - in' and a hid - in',
jive. ___ Oh ___ big con - niv - er, noth - in' but a jiv - er,
ren - der, Oh ___ Ma - lin - da, she's a sol - id send - er,
go. ___ Slip - pin' and a - slid - in', peep - in' and a hid - in',
C7
G7
been told a long time a - go. ___ I've been told, _ ba - by,
done got ___ hip to your jive. ___ Slip - pin' and __ slid - in',
you know you bet - ter sur - ren - der, Slip - pin' and __ slid - in',
been told a long time a - go. ___ I've been told, _ ba - by,
F7
C7
1,2,3
4
You've been bold _ I won't be your fool no more.
Peep-in' and hid - in' won't be your fool no more.
Peep-in' and hid - in' won't be your fool no more.
You've been bold _ I won't be your fool no more.
rit.

RIP IT UP

Words and Music by ROBERT A. BLACKWELL
and JOHN S. MARASCALCO

Copyright © 1956, Renewed 1984 Venice Music Inc.
All Rights Controlled and Administered by EMI BLACKWOOD MUSIC INC. under license from ATV MUSIC (VENICE)
All Rights Reserved International Copyright Secured Used by Permission

I'm gon - na rock it up!
I'm gon - na
C9
shake it up!
G
I'm gon - na ball it up!
D7
C7
1 G
I'm gon - na rip it up!
and ball to night.
D7
2 G
C9
G
2. I night.
3. A -

DON'T BE CRUEL
(To A Heart That's True)

Words and Music by OTIS BLACKWELL
and ELVIS PRESLEY

Copyright © 1956 by Elvis Presley Music and Unart Music Corp.
Copyright Renewed
Elvis Presley Music administered throughout the world by Unichappell Music, Inc. (Rightsong Music, Publisher)
International Copyright Secured All Rights Reserved
Unauthorized copying, arranging, adapting, recording or public performance is an infringement of copyright.
Infringers are liable under the law.

2
C
F
G7
true.
I don't want no oth - er love,
F
G7
C
C
Ba - by, it's just you I'm think - ing of.
Don't stop think - ing
walk up to the
C7
F
of me Don't make me feel this way,
preach - er, and let us say, "I do."
Come on o - ver here and
Then you'll know you
C
Dm7
love me, You know what I want you to say. Don't Be Cruel
have me, And I'll know I'll have you too. Don't Be Cruel
G7
C
F
to a heart that's true.
to a heart that's true.
Why should we be a -
I don't want no oth - er

G7 F G7 C
part? I real - ly love you, ba - by, cross my heart
love, Ba - by it's just you I'm think - ing
C Dm7
Let's of. Don't Be Cruel
G7 C Dm7
to a heart that's true. Don't Be Cruel
G7 C C7 F
to a heart that's true. I don't want no oth - er
G7 F G7 C C7
love Ba - by, it's just you I'm think-ing of.

HOUND DOG

Words and Music by JERRY LEIBER
and MIKE STOLLER

Medium Rock
f
B7
Bb7
You ain't noth - in' but a Hound Dog, cry - in' all the
f
E7
Eb7
time. You ain't noth - in' but a Hound Dog,

Copyright © by Elvis Presley Music & Lion Publishing Company, Inc.
Copyright renewed, assigned to Gladys Music (Administered 1956 by Chappell & Co., Intersong Music, Publisher) and MCA MUSIC PUBLISHING, A Division of MCA INC.
All rights for the U.S.A. controlled by Chappell & Co. (Intersong Music, Publisher)
International Copyright Secured All Rights Reserved
Unauthorized copying, arranging, adapting, recording or public performance is an infringement of copyright.
Infringers are liable under the law.

B7
Bb7
cry - in' all the time.
Well, you ain't
F7 F#7
Eb7 E7
nev - er caught a rab - bit and you ain't no friend of
Bb B
(tacet)
Bb7 B7
mine.
When they said you was high - classed,
well, that was just a lie.
When they said you was

E7
Eb7
high - classed,
Well, that was just a
Bb B
lie.
Well, you ain't
F7 F#7
Eb7 E7
1 Bb B
ne - ver caught a rab - bit and you ain't no friend of mine
(tacet)
2 Bb B
Eb7 E7
Bb B
You ain't noth - in' but a mine.
ped.

THE GREEN DOOR

Words and Music by BOB DAVIE
and MARVIN MOORE

Copyright © 1956 by Alley Music Corporation and Trio Music Company, Inc.
Copyright Renewed
All rights administered by Hudson Bay Music, Inc.
International Copyright Secured All Rights Reserved
Used by Permission

D
A
There's an old pi - a - no and they play it hot__ be-hind the green door._
Saw an eye - ball peep - in' thru a smok - y cloud_ be-hind the green door._
D
A
Don't know what they're do - in' but they laugh a lot__ be-hind the green door._
When I said Joe sent_ me some-one laughed out loud_ be-hind the green door._
E7
D7
Wish they'd let me in___ so I could find out what's_ be - hind the
All I want to do___ is join the hap - py crew___ be - hind the
1
A
green door._
2
A
A13
green door._

BLUEBERRY HILL

Words and Music by AL LEWIS,
LARRY STOCK and VINCENT ROSE

Copyright © 1940 by Chappell & Co.
Copyright Renewed, Assigned to Chappell & Co. and Sovereign Music Corp.
International Copyright Secured All Rights Reserved
Unauthorized copying, arranging, adapting, recording or public performance is an infringement of copyright.
Infringers are liable under the law.

Eb
Db7
Eb
Ab6
Eb
Eb6
my dreams came true. The wind in the wil - low played
mp
Ebmaj7
Ab6
Eb
Eb6
Eb7
D7
Gm
D7
Love's sweet mel - o - dy; But all of those vows we made
cresc.
Gm
D7
G
Bb7
Eb7
Ab
Were nev - er to be. Tho' we're a - part, You're part of me
p
Eb
Bb7
still For you were my thrill On Blue - ber - ry
1
Eb
Db7
Eb
Eb7
2
Eb
Ab6
Eb
Hill. I found my Hill.
mf
mp

LET THE GOOD TIMES ROLL

Words and Music by LEONARD LE[illegible]

Copyright © 1956 Atlantic Music Corp.
Copyright Renewed 1984
International Copyright Secured All Rights Reserved

hold you tight, tell me ev-'ry-thing is right to night;
paint the town, don't let noth-in' ev-er bring us down;
cra-zy fling, love can be such a swing-in' thing;
B♭
F
C7
Come on, ba-by, let the good times roll, roll on and
1 F
2,3 F
B♭
F
on. on. Feel so good
Feel so good
C7
F
B♭
F
in my arms, Sug-ar ba-by,
when you're close, Sug-ar ba-by,

G7
C7
F
you're my good luck charm.
I dig you the most.
Come on, ba - by, let the
good times roll,
come on, ba - by, let me thrill your soul;
B♭
F
F7
To Coda
come on, ba - by, let the good times roll,
roll on and
F
D.S. al Coda
on.
CODA
F
on.

SINCE I MET YOU BABY

Words and Music by
IVORY JOE HUNTER

Slow Blues

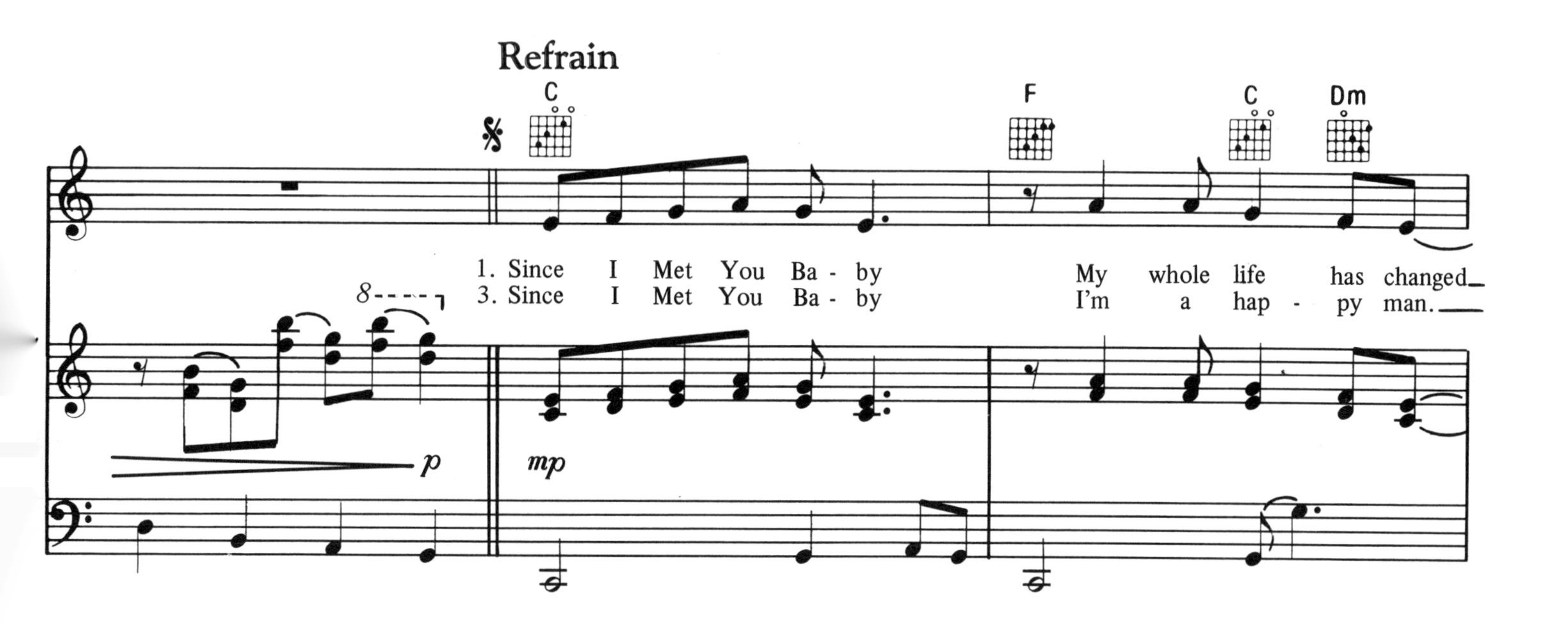

Copyright © 1956 by Progressive Music Publishing Co., Inc.
Copyright Renewed, all rights controlled by Unichappell Music, Inc. (Rightsong Music, Publisher)
International Copyright Secured All Rights Reserved
Unauthorized copying, arranging, adapting, recording or public performance is an infringement of copyright.
Infringers are liable under the law.

C
C7
F
Since I Met You Ba - by
Since I Met You Ba - by
My whole life has changed.
I'm a hap py - man.
C
And
I'm
G7
ev - 'ry - bod - y tells me
gon- na try to please you
that I am not the
in ev - 'ry way I
1 C
same.
G7
To 2nd Refrain
2 C
can.
G7
C
Fine
p
mf

Refrain
C
F
C
Dm
C
mp
2. I don't need no - bod - y to tell my trou - bles to,
C7
F
I don't need no - bod - y to tell my trou - bles to,
C
G7
'Cause Since I Met You Ba - by
C
G7
D.S. al Fine
all I need is you.
p

LUCILLE

Words and Music by RICHARD PENNIMA
and ALBERT COLLI

© 1957, 1960 (Renewed 1985, 1988) VENICE MUSIC, INC.
All Rights Controlled and Administered by EMI BLACKWOOD MUSIC INC. under licence from ATV MUSIC (VENICE)
All Rights Reserved International Copyright Secured Used by Permission

C7
cille, won't you do your sis - ter's
cille, please come back where you be -
cille, ba - by, sat - is - fy my
F7
will? Oh, Lu - cille,
long. Oh, Lu - cille,
heart. Oh, Lu - cille,
C7
won't you do your sis - ter's will?
please come back where you be - long.
ba - by, sat - is - fy my heart.
G7
Well, you ran a - way and left,
I been good to you, ba - by.
I slaved for you, ba - by, and

F7
C7
I love you still.
Please don't leave me a - lone.
gave you such a won - der - ful start.
1,2
3
Lu -
Lu -
I
woke up this morn - ing, Lu - cille was not in sight. I
asked her friends a - bout her, but all their lips were tight. Lu -

F7
cille,
please come back where you be -
C7
G7
long.
I been good to you, ba - by.
F7
C7
Please don't leave me a - lone.

ALL SHOOK UP

Words and Music by OTIS BLACKWELL
and ELVIS PRESLEY

Copyright © 1957 Unart Music Corp.
Copyright Renewed
All rights administered by Unart Music Corp. and Unichappell Music, Inc.
(Rightsong Music, Publisher)
International Copyright Secured All Rights Reserved
Unauthorized copying, arranging, adapting, recording or public performance is an infringement of copyright.
Infringers are liable under the law.

hands are sha - ky and my knees are weak. I can't seem to stand on my
own two feet, Who do you thank when you have such luck? I'm in
E♭7
F7
love! I'm all shook up! Mm mm oh, oh, yeah,
B♭
E♭7
B♭
E♭7
yeah!
1. Please don't ask what's on my mind, I'm a
2. Tongue gets tied when I try to speak, My

B♭
E♭7
lit - tle mixed up but I'm feel - in' fine When I'm near that girl that
in - sides shake like a leaf on a tree, There's on - ly one cure for this
F7
I love best, My heart beats so it scares me to death!
soul of mine, That's to have the girl that I love so fine!
She
B♭
touched my hand, What a chill I got, Her kiss - es are like a vol
ca - no that's hot! I'm proud to say she's my but - ter - cup, I'm in'

E♭7
F7
love! I'm all shook up! Mm mm oh, oh, yeah,
1
B♭
E♭7
B♭
yeah!
2. My
2
B♭
yeah! I'm all shook up! Mm
E♭7
F7
B♭
mm oh, oh, yeah, yeah! I'm all shook up! Mm
E♭7
F7
B♭
mm oh, oh, yeah, yeah! I'm all shook up!

SEARCHIN'

Words and Music by JERRY LEIBER
and MIKE STOLLER

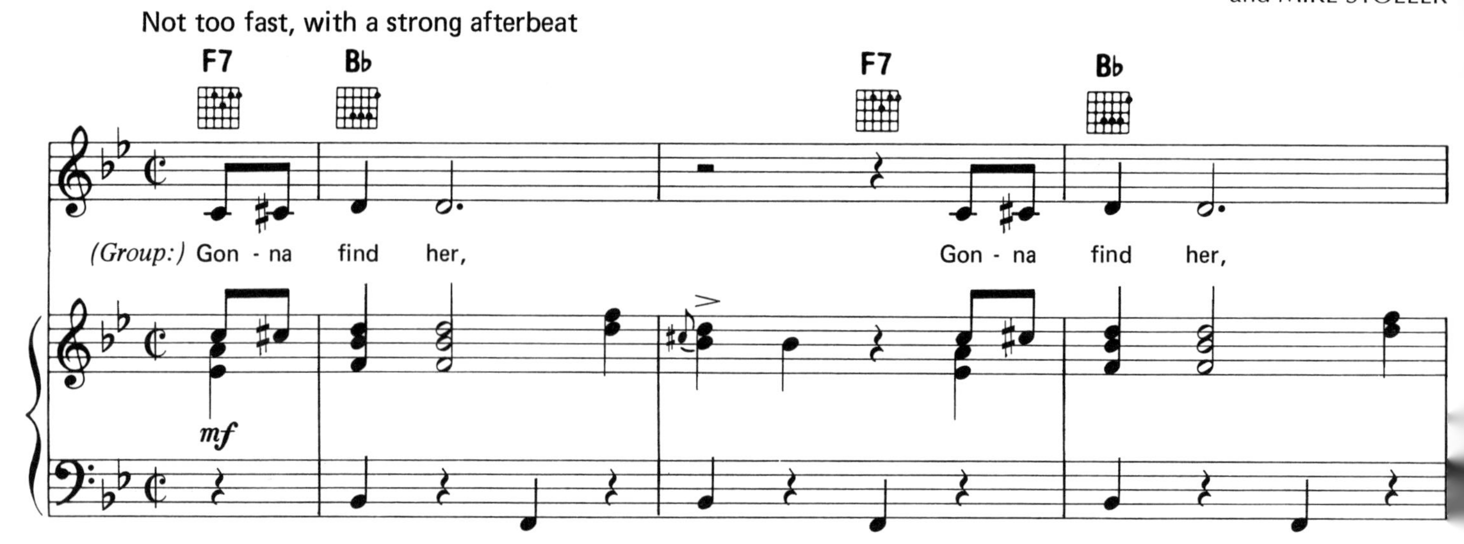

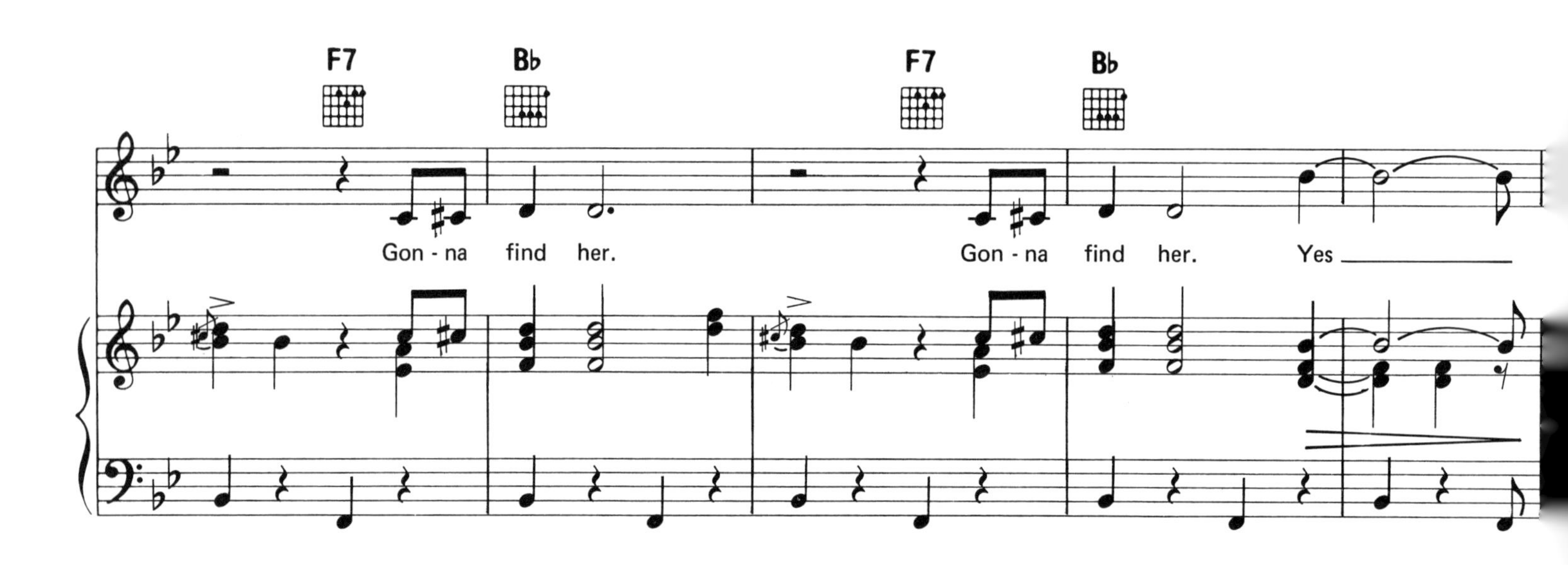

Copyright © 1957 by Tiger Music, Inc.
Copyright renewed, assigned to Chappell & Co. (Intersong Music, Publisher), Quintet Music, Inc. and Bienstock Publishing Co.
All rights Administered by Chappell & Co.
International Copyright Secured All Rights Reserved
Unauthorized copying, arranging, adapting, recording or public performance is an infringement of copyright.
Infringers are liable under the law.

Eb7
Bb
Bb7
search - in' ev - 'ry which a - way yeah yeah, Oh yes,
Eb9
Bb
search - in' search - in' search - in' ev - 'ry
mf
Eb7
Bb
F7
which a - way yeah yeah, but I'm like the North - west Mount - ie
mp
Bb
Guitar Tacet
F7
Bb
F7
Bb
you know I'll bring her in some day.
(Group:) Gon-na find her. (Group:) Gon-na find her.
mf

Well now if I have to swim a riv-er, you know I will and
Sher-lock Holmes Sam Spade got noth-ing, child, on me
if I have to climb a moun-tain you know I will and
Sar-geant Fri-day, Char-lie Chan and Bos-ton Black-ie. No
if she's hid-ing up on a blue-ber-ry hill
mat-ter where she's hid-ing she's gon-na hear me com-ing I'm gon-na
Eb9
Eb7
Bb
Cm7
am I gon-na find her, child, you know I will. 'Cause I've been
walk right down that street like Bull-dog Drum-mond. 'Cause I've been
mp

Eb9
Bb
search - in'
Oh, yeah search - in'
Oh, Lord
My good - ness
Um child
search - in' ev - 'ry
mf
Eb7
Bb
F7
F7+5
which a - way yeah yeah, but I'm like the North - west Mount - ie.
mp
Bb
Guitar Tacet
F7
1 Bb
F7
Bb
You know I'll bring her in some day.
(Group:) Gon-na find her.
(Group:) Gon-na find her.
2 Bb
F7
Bb
Well, day.
find her.
(Group:) Gon-na find her.
mf
dim. poco a poco
ppp

OVER THE MOUNTAIN, ACROSS THE SEA

Words and Music by
REX GARVIN

Copyright © 1957 (Renewed) by Arc Corp.
All Rights Reserved

F
Dm
Gm7
C7
She's passed the winds that's blow - ing loud; — o - ver the moun-tain, a
girl waits for me, —
Tell all the sands and ev - 'ry blade of grass, — please tell the winds to
let my love pass; — o - ver the moun-tain, a girl waits for
G7

F
B♭
F
F7
B♭
me.
Tell the moon up
F
in the sky,
tell the birds that fly by, that
G7
Dm7/A
B♭dim
G7/B
o - ver and o - ver and o - ver the moun - tain, my
C7
Gm7/D
E♭dim
C7/E
love waits for me.

F
Dm
Gm7
C7
In - to each dark and star - ry night,
Oh, what a mys - ter - y that's sealed so tight,
o - ver the moun - tain a girl waits for me.
1 F
Dm
Gm7
C7
2 F
B♭
F
me.
rall.

(Let Me Be Your)
TEDDY BEAR

Words and Music by KAL MANN
and BERNIE LOWE

Medium Bright Rock

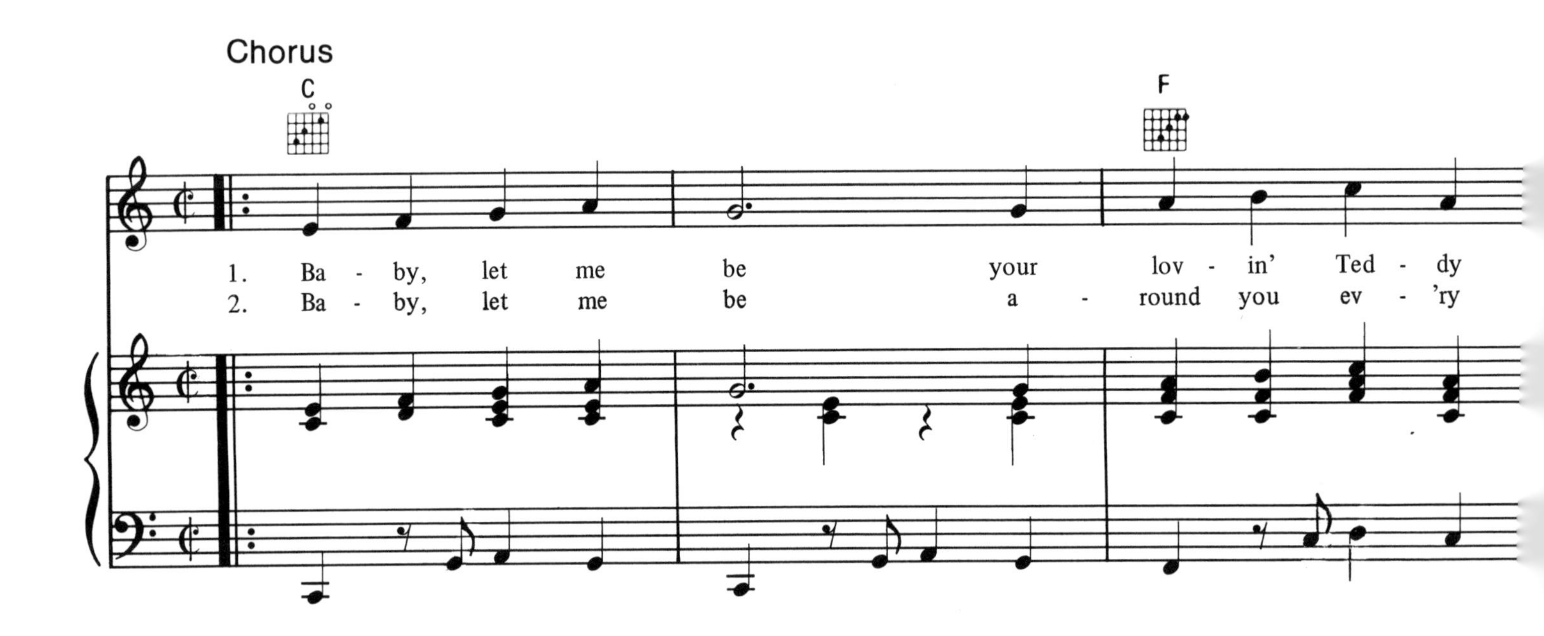
Chorus
C
F
1. Ba - by, let me be your lov - in' Ted - dy
2. Ba - by, let me be a - round you ev - 'ry

C
F
Bear. Put a chain a - round my neck and
night. Run your fin - gers through my hair and

Copyright © 1957 by Gladys Music, Inc.
Copyright Renewed
All Rights Controlled by Chappell & Co. (Intersong Music, Publisher)
International Copyright Secured All Rights Reserved
Unauthorized copying, arranging, adapting, recording or public performance is an infringement of copyright.
Infringers are liable under the law.

C
G7
lead me an - y - where.
cud - dle me real tight.
Oh let me be
(Tacet)
your Ted - dy Bear.
C
I
F
G7
don't want to be your ti - ger 'cause ti - gers play too rough.
I
don't want to be your li - on 'cause li - ons ain't the kind you love e -

C
(Tacet)
C
nough. Just wan - na be your Ted - dy
Bear.
F
Put a chain a - round my neck and
C
G7
(Tacet)
lead me an - y - where. Oh, let me be your Ted-dy
1
C
F7
G7
Bear.
2
C
F7
C
Bear.

WHOLE LOTTA SHAKIN' GOIN' ON

Words and Music by SUNNY DAVID
and DAVID WILLIAMS

Copyright © 1958 Cherio Corp. & Copar Music, Inc.
Copyright Renewed
International Copyright Secured All Rights Reserved

D7
Ain't no - bod - y fak - in',
G
Whole lot - ta shak - in' goin' on.
C7
Come on o - ver ba - by,
G
Whole lot - ta kick - in' in the barn,
C7
Come on o - ver ba

G
- by,
We got the bull by the
horn,
D7
Ev - 'ry - thing is tak - in',
Whole lot - ta shak - in' goin' on.
1 G
2 G
D7
Em7
D7
G6

JAILHOUSE ROCK

Words and Music by JERRY LEIBER
and MIKE STOLLER

© 1957 (Renewed) by Mike Stoller Music and Jerry Leiber Music
All Rights Administered by WB Music Corp.
All Rights Reserved

F7(#9)
(tacet)
E7
band was jump - in' and the joint be - gan to swing. You
drum - mer boy from Il - lin - ois went crash, boom, bang: The
sure would be de - light - ed with your com - pa - ny. Come
F7(#9)
(tacet)
should - 've heard those knocked - out jail - birds sing.
whole rhy - thm sec - tion was the pur - ple gang. Let's
on and do the Jail - house Rock with me.
Bb7
rock! Let's
ff
F7
rock! Ev - 'ry -

4. The sad sack was a-sittin' on a block of stone,
   Way over in the corner weeping all alone.
   The warden said: Hey, buddy, don't you be no square.
   If you can't find a partner, use a wooden chair!
   Let's rock, etc.

5. Shifty Henry said to Bugs: For Heaven's sake,
   No one's lookin'; now's our chance to make a break.
   Bugsy turned to Shifty and he said: Nix, nix;
   I wanna stick around a while and get my kicks,
   Let's rock, etc.

SILHOUETTES

Words and Music by FRANK C. SLAY JR.
and BOB CREWE

Slow beat tempo
mf
F Dm Gm C7 F Dm Gm C7
Took a walk and passed your house late last night, All the shades were pulled and drawn 'way down
mp
F Dm Gm C7 F Dm
tight; From with-in a dim light cast two sil-hou-ettes on the shade, Oh what a love - ly
Gm C7 F Dm Gm C7 F Dm
cou-ple they made. Put {his her} arms a-round your waist, held you tight, Kiss-es I could al-most

Copyright © 1957 (Renewed) Regent Music Corporation
All Rights Reserved

Gm C7 F Dm Gm C7
taste in the night, Won-dered why I'm not the {guy girl} whose sil-hou-ette's on the
F Dm Gm C7 F C7 F Dm Gm C7
shade I could-n't hide the tears in my eyes Ah,
F D7 Gm C7 F D7 G Em Am D7
Lost con-trol, and rang your bell, I was
G Em Am D7 G Em
sore, "Let me in, or else I'll beat down your door." When two stran-gers, who had

Am D7 G Em Am D7 G Em
been two sil-hou-ettes on the shade said to my shock "You're on the *wrong* block" Rushed down to your house with
Am D7 G Em Am D7 G Em
wings on my feet, Loved you like I've nev-er loved you my sweet, Vowed that you and I would
Am D7 G Em Am D7 G D7
be two sil-hou-ettes on the shade *All* of our days, two sil-hou-ettes on the shade.
For Repeat
Fine
G Em Am D7 G E7 Am D7 Am D7 G
Ah,
Fade out repeat ad lib.

RAUNCHY

Words and Music by WILLIAM JUSTIS
and SIDNEY MANKER

Copyright © 1957 by Hi-Lo Music, Inc. Copyright Renewed
Printed in the U.S.A. by Unichappell Music, Inc.
Internatational Copyright Secured All Rights Reserved
Unauthorized copying, arranging, adapting, recording or public performance is an infringement of copyright.
Infringers are liable under the law.

D
2
3
3
G7
D
A7
G7
3
3
D
3
G7
3
3
3
3

D
A7
G9
D
3
4
G7
D
A7
G7

D
D.S. al Coda
CODA
G
D
A7
G7
D
Repeat and Fade

DIZZY MISS LIZZIE

Words and Music by
LARRY WILLIAMS

Copyright © 1958 VENICE MUSIC
Copyright Renewed, ARC MUSIC CORP. for the United States.
International Copyright Secured All Rights Reserved

E7
A
1. You make me diz - zy, Miss Liz - zie, the way you rock and roll.
2. You make me diz - zy, Miss Liz - zie, when you call my name.
3. Run and tell your ma - ma I want you to be my bride.
D
You make me diz - zy, Miss Liz zie,
Woo, ba - by,
Run and tell your broth - er,
A
when you do the Stroll.
say you're driv - ing me in - sane.
ba - by don't run and hide.

E
Come on, Miss Liz - zie,
Come on, come on, come on, come on, ba - by, I
You make me diz - zy, Miss Liz - zie, girl,

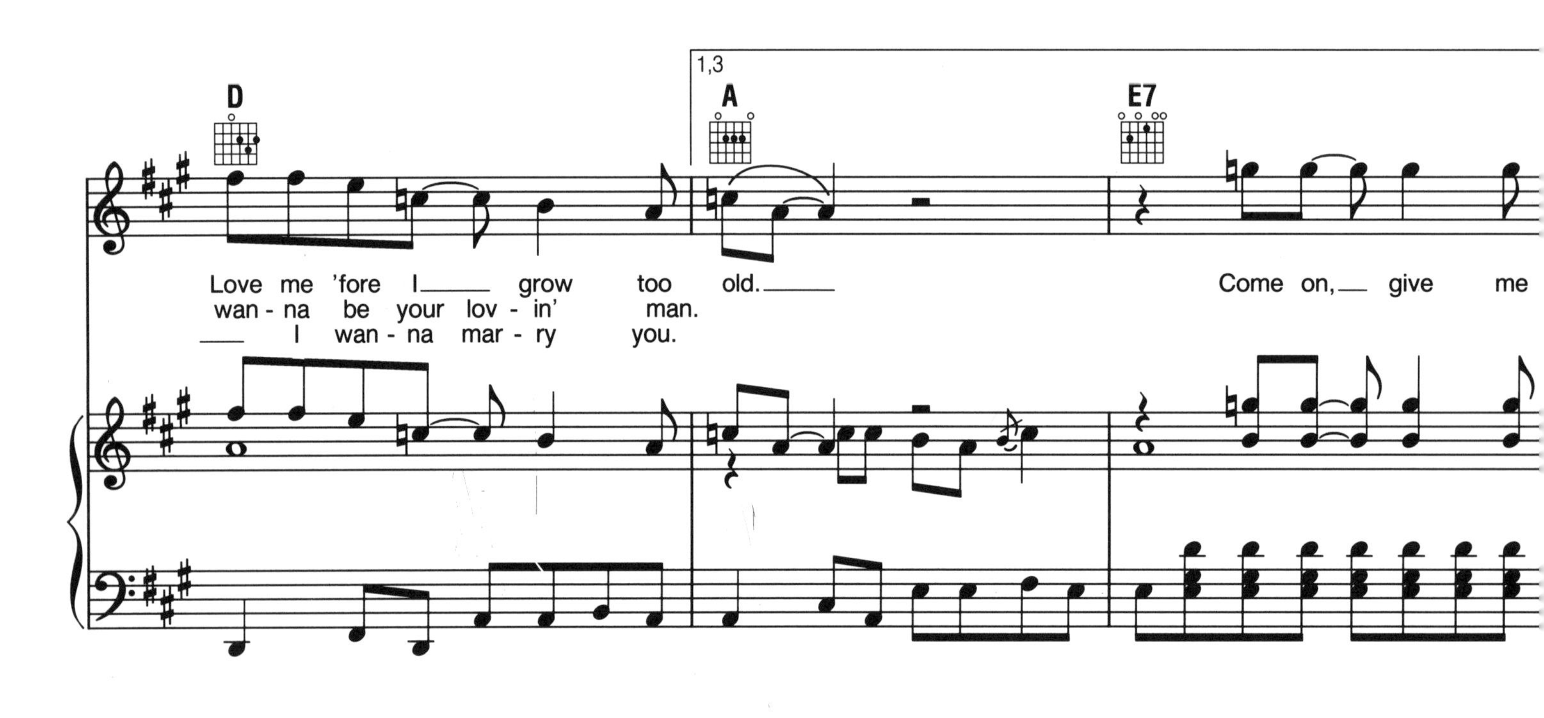
D
1,3
A
E7
Love me 'fore I grow too old.
wan - na be your lov - in' man.
I wan - na mar - ry you.
Come on, give me

A
fe - ver,
put your lit - tle hand in mine.

D
You make me diz - zy, Miss Liz - zie,
3rd diz - zy
Oh, girl, you look so
A
E
fine.
Just a rock - in' and a - roll - in'
You're just a rock - in' and a - roll - in'
D
A
E7
To Coda
Girl, I said I wish you were mine.
Oo, I said I wish you were mine.
(Shriek) OW!
2
A
E7
D.S. al Coda
(man.)
(Shriek) OW!
CODA
A

BONY MORONIE

Words and Music by
LARRY WILLIAMS

Copyright © 1957, 1967, Renewed 1985 VENICE MUSIC CORPORATION for the World except the United States
© Renewed by ARC MUSIC CORP. for the United States only.
All Rights for Canada Controlled and Administered by EMI BLACKWOOD MUSIC INC.
All Rights reserved Used by Permission

B♭7
see her rock with her blue jeans on.
We'll get mar - ried on a night in June.
F
She's not fat she's just skin
And rock and roll by the light of the
F7
and bones.
sil - v'ry moon,
C
I love her,
B♭
she loves me.
C
Oh, how hap - py now
B♭
we can be. Mak - ing

F7
love un - der - neath the ap - ple tree.
1 B♭
F
2 B♭
F
2. Well, I
I got a girl,
C
B♭
A♭
G
I got a girl,
G6
She's my one, she's my on - ly she's m

G7
G
heart's de - sire,
She's a real up -
G6
G7
set - ter she's
real live wire.
Ev - 'ry -
C
C7
bod - y looks
when she
goes
by.
G
She's
a
real good,
good girl
real - ly

G7
D
grabs your eyes.
I love her,
C
D
C
she loves me.
Oh, how hap - py now
we can be.
Mak - ing
G7
love un - der - neath
the ap - ple tree.
C
G
D
I got a girl,
I got a girl.